T0130381

MY BLENDED FAMILY

AN ADOPTION STORY

CHINWE LUCIA EGBE

AuthorHouse™
1663 Liberty Drive
Bloomington, IN 47403
www.authorhouse.com
Phone: 833-262-8899

Because of the dynamic nature of the Internet, any web addresses or links contained in this book may have changed
since publication and may no longer be valid. The views expressed in this work are solely those of the author and do
not necessarily reflect the views of the publisher, and the publisher hereby disclaims any responsibility for them.

Any people depicted in stock imagery provided by Getty Images are models,
and such images are being used for illustrative purposes only.
Certain stock imagery © Getty Images.

This book is printed on acid-free paper.

ISBN: 978-1-6655-3545-8 (sc)
ISBN: 978-1-6655-3546-5 (e)

Library of Congress Control Number: 2021916962

Print information available on the last page.

Published by AuthorHouse 08/18/2021

authorHOUSE®

MY BLENDED
FAMILY

Preface

This book is adapted from true-life experiences. It is equipped with illustrations and interactive wordings to enhance each user's experience. This book is targeted at families who are considering or are in the process of adopting or who have already adopted a baby. Various issues may arise during each of these periods which may become very trying for the family. It is my hope that this book will guide parents on child identity problems and how to answer questions that arise while easing into a new family unit.

Joyful reading!
Dr. Chinwe Lucia Egbe

To deny adoption loss is to deny the emotional reality of everyone involved.
—Sherrie Eldridge

Meet my family

My name is Adaeze, a name meaning 'daughter of a king'. Mum chose that name for me because she always called me a princess. Today I am three years old.

My mummy is beautiful. She is called Nneoma.

I have the best brother in the whole world. He is called Nwachi. He dotes on me.

Note for Parents

Help your child identify everyone who makes up their direct family. Make a list of their names and keep it for the family tree later. This personalisation of family members—*my* brother, *my* dad, *my* sister—gives them a sense of belonging.

When was I born?

Adaeze was born in eastern Nigeria, same as her adopted mum. In the eastern part of Nigeria, there are lots of beautiful fruits, like *udala* and soursop, and they make lovely food from *a vegetable called okra. Mum made this and I love eating it* with fufu.

Mum tells me I was born on a Thursday evening, a cool night as she describes it. The weather was perfect for the birth of a princess.

Note for Parents

Tell your kids only their real birth story. If you don't know their birth story, then stick to Adaeze's birth story and make your own paintings.

Why did you choose me?

After I realised I was adopted, I have sometimes asked myself why Mum choose me. There are so many other kids she would have picked, so why me?

Can you please help me understand? Why me?

Note for Parents

You may want to tell your child that it was love at first sight. 'I loved everything about you from the day I saw you.'

You were not seeking any features (in appearance or otherwise), but you loved your child immediately.

Tell your child that this has been the best decision of your life.

My unique family

Mum tells me that I have many aunts and uncles. Tall ones, short ones, funny ones, weird ones.

I remember Aunty Blessing. She made funny faces. She tried feeding me once, and we both really struggled. I just wouldn't keep my head still, and she couldn't keep up and almost slipped the feeder in my nose!

Let's look at my family tree. Can you spot me?

Can you see Nwachi?

Can you draw your family tree?

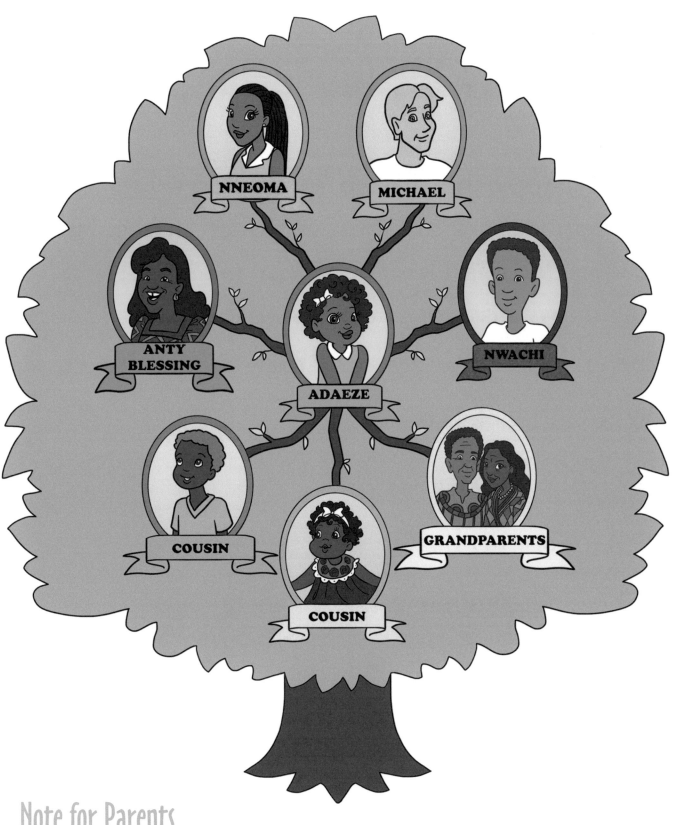

Note for Parents

Use your scrapbook to draw your baby's family tree.

Find interesting stories, expanding the tree as you go along.

Embracing my uniqueness

I feel happy that I have a very large family. But Nwachi looks a bit like everyone! He's got eyes like his daddy's. He's got natural piercings, as mum and one of his aunties do. He laughs like his second aunty. He's funny like Aunty Blessing.

Who do I look like?

Whose eyes do I have?

Where are my birthmarks?

Who sings like me in the family?

Why am I able to drum?

Note for Parents

This is a difficult, but fun page to let your child embrace their uniqueness.

All babies are born unique. Their uniqueness develops over time. Some similarities can be found with family members, and others can't—they are unique!

Identify the child's uniqueness and link it to a beautiful talent. You see Adaeze asking why she's able to drum. Not everyone in the family can, so Adaeze has got a unique talent.

Where's my daddy?

I see Nwachi going to his daddy every other weekend. Why can't I go with him? Why can't I see my daddy? Mummy says she is my only parent because our family broke up before I was born. She tells me it's not my fault and that sometimes adults break up, but she will never stop loving me.

I believe her!

Do you have a mum and a dad?

Do they love you?

Note for Parents

Use this section to explain your unique family. Tell your child that some families have two dads, two mums, one dad, or one mum.

Pick yours and make it beautiful. The suggestion here, is to identify a role model for your child and allow the child to visit them when their sibling visits their other parent. That way, both kids have the same opportunity to visit with an extended family or friend outside the home

Use this opportunity to describe 'blended family' to your child. Explain how each family unit is different. No two families are ever the same.

My birth parents

My mum has explained to me that I was adopted, so I know. Although I am very happy, I still wish to know my birth parents someday

Will my mummy help me find them?

Will I ever find them?

Will it be worth it?

Will I still want to find them when I'm an adult?

Note for Parents

You are encouraged to tell your child from the outset that they were adopted.

Tell them that you can help them find their birth parents only if you know where to find them. Constantly reassure your baby of your love even during the search.

About the Author

The author is an adoptee currently finalising the adoption process of her daughter. The consideration of adoption started over ten years ago but she couldn't really act on it as she was trying to have other children through the process of IVF, which she did severally, without success.

Things were put in better perspective during her mum's battle with cancer when she travelled to Nigeria, to put her mum's estate in order. They had a deep conversation about the failed IVFs and her mum insisted she adopts instead of putting my life at risk and it would be the chance to have the baby I've always wanted.

The experience to write this book came about through the adoption journey. The author is a Senior Lecturer in Accounting at Nottingham Business School, Nottingham Trent University with a PhD in Accounting obtained from the University of Reading. Actively engages in Instagram, Facebook and Twitter with active followers. The author is an active researcher in the field of accounting and finance, but has personal experience gained in adoption which has prompted the writing of this story book. Affiliated with the IAC- the international adoption agency through which the author was able to adopt her child.

Printed in the United States
by Baker & Taylor Publisher Services